JAMAICA BAY MARSH ISLAND RESTORATION

JAMAICA BAY MARSH ISLAND RESTORATION

STRUCTURES OF COASTAL RESILIENCE
Jamaica Bay Team
Spitzer School of Architecture
The City College of New York

Catherine Seavitt Nordenson, editor
Associate Professor of Landscape Architecture

Kjirsten Alexander
Research Associate

Danae Alessi
Research Associate

Eli Sands
Research Assistant

JAMAICA BAY PAMPHLET LIBRARY
15 Jamaica Bay Marsh Island Restoration

ISBN 978-1-942900-15-3

CONTACT
Catherine Seavitt Nordenson
cseavittnordenson@ccny.cuny.edu
www.structuresofcoastalresilience.org

SCR Jamaica Bay Team
The City College of New York
Spitzer School of Architecture
Program in Landscape Architecture, Room 2M24A
141 Convent Avenue New York, New York 10031

COVER
Jamaica Bay high tide at dawn, 2014.
photo: Catherine Seavitt

supported by

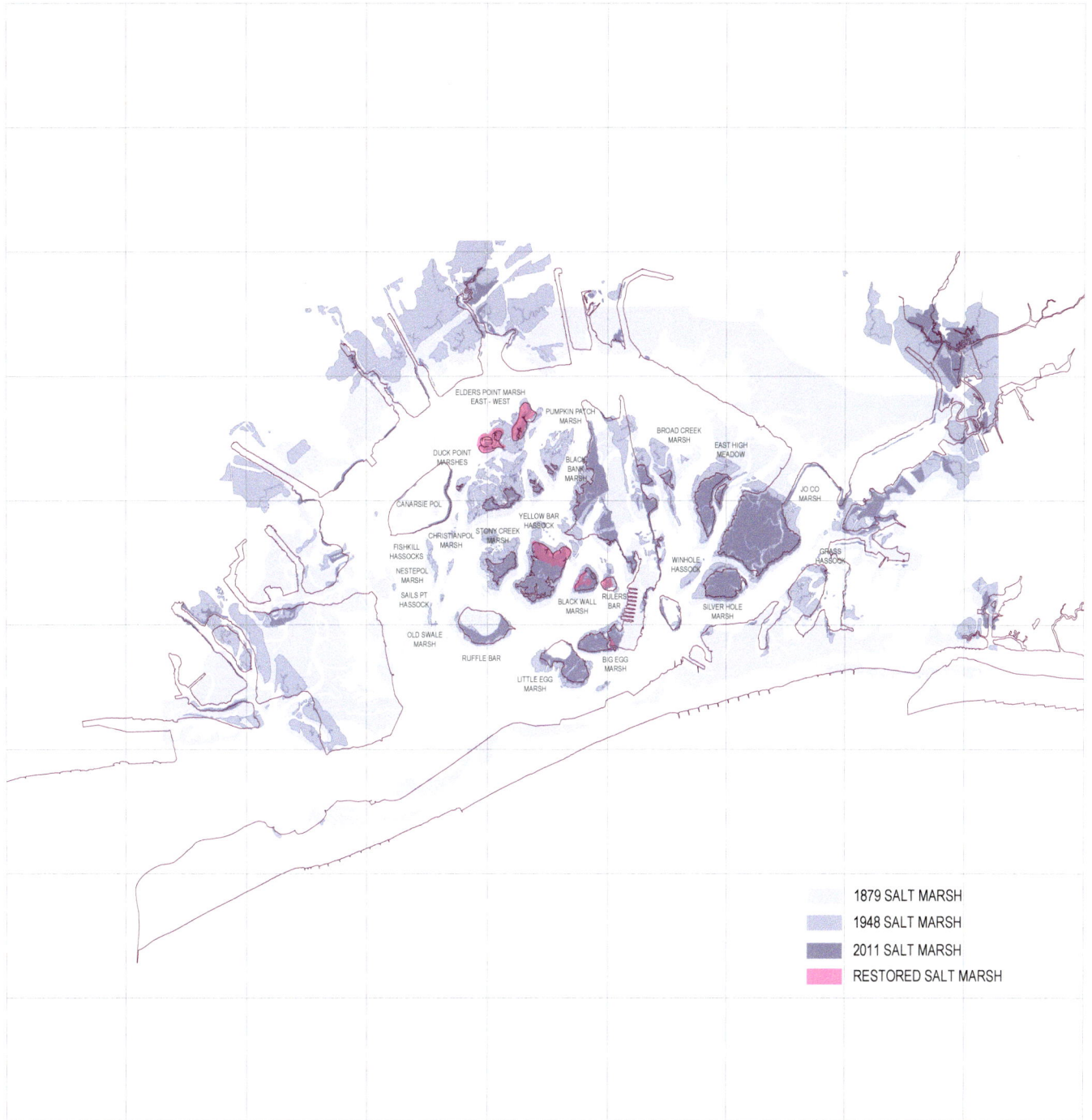

ELDERS POINT MARSH
EAST - WEST

PUMPKIN PATCH
MARSH

DUCK POINT
MARSHES

BLACK
BANK
MARSH

BROAD CREEK
MARSH

EAST HIGH
MEADOW

CANARSIE POL

YELLOW BAR
HASSOCK

JO CO
MARSH

CHRISTIANPOL
MARSH

STONY CREEK
MARSH

FISHKILL
HASSOCKS

NESTEPOL
MARSH

WINHOLE
HASSOCK

GRASS
HASSOCK

SAILS PT
HASSOCK

RULERS
BAR

BLACK WALL
MARSH

SILVER HOLE
MARSH

OLD SWALE
MARSH

RUFFLE BAR

BIG EGG
MARSH

LITTLE EGG
MARSH

	1879 SALT MARSH
	1948 SALT MARSH
	2011 SALT MARSH
	RESTORED SALT MARSH

SHORELINE 1929
CHANNELS 1929
MUDFLATS 1929
INFRASTRUCTURE
SHORELINE 1879
CHANNELS 1879
MUDFLATS 1879
INFRASTRUCTURE

Historic edge and channel evolution 1879-1929

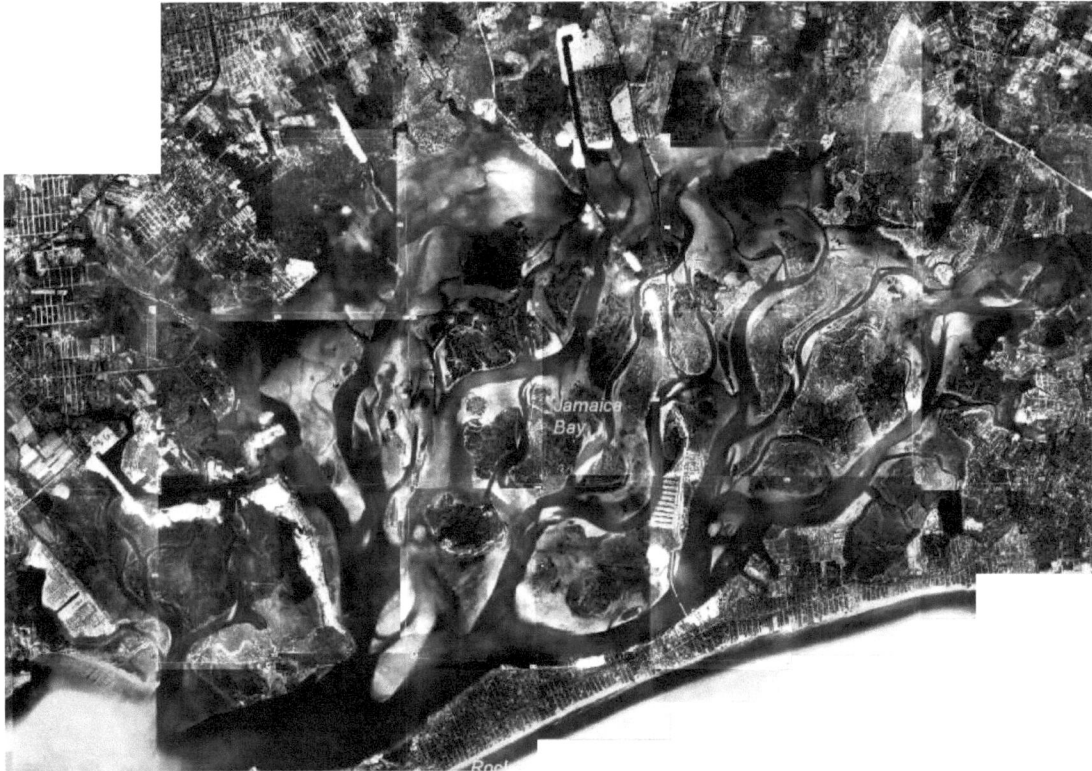

Aerial imagery at Jamaica Bay, 1924
image source: NYC DoITT Map

SCALE COMPARISON

JAMAICA BAY

BROAD CHANNEL
~1200 ACRES

13.4 MILES

MANHATTAN

CENTRAL PARK
843 ACRES

MARSH ISLAND ACREAGE CALCULATED AT MEAN TIDE (0' NAVD88)

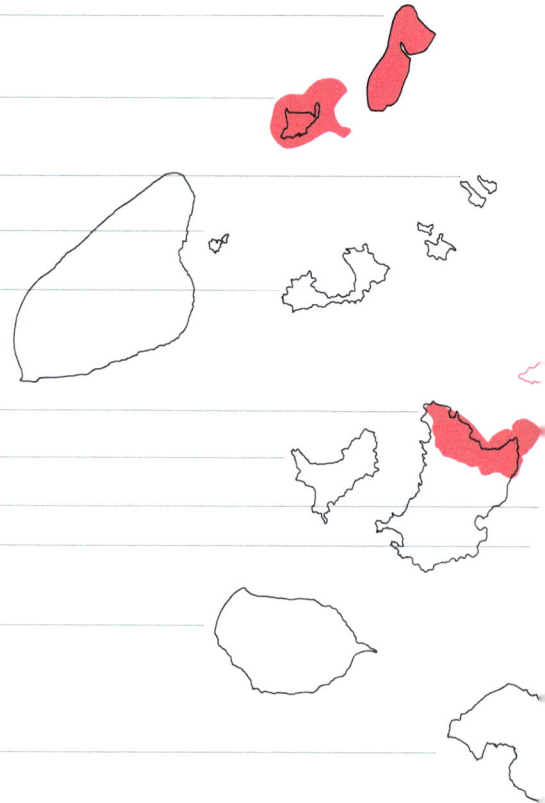

ELDERS POINT EAST 43 ACRES RESTORED

ELDERS POINT WEST 40 ACRES RESTORED

PUMPKIN PATCH 10 ACRES

CHRISTIAN POL 2 ACRES

DUCK POINT 29 ACRES

CANARSIE POL 280 ACRES

YELLOW BAR 141 ACRES (46 RESTORED)

STONY CREEK 39 ACRES

RULERS BAR 10 ACRES RESTORED

BLACK WALL 31 ACRES (20 RESTORED)

RUFFLE BAR 131 ACRES

LITTLE EGG 103 ACRES

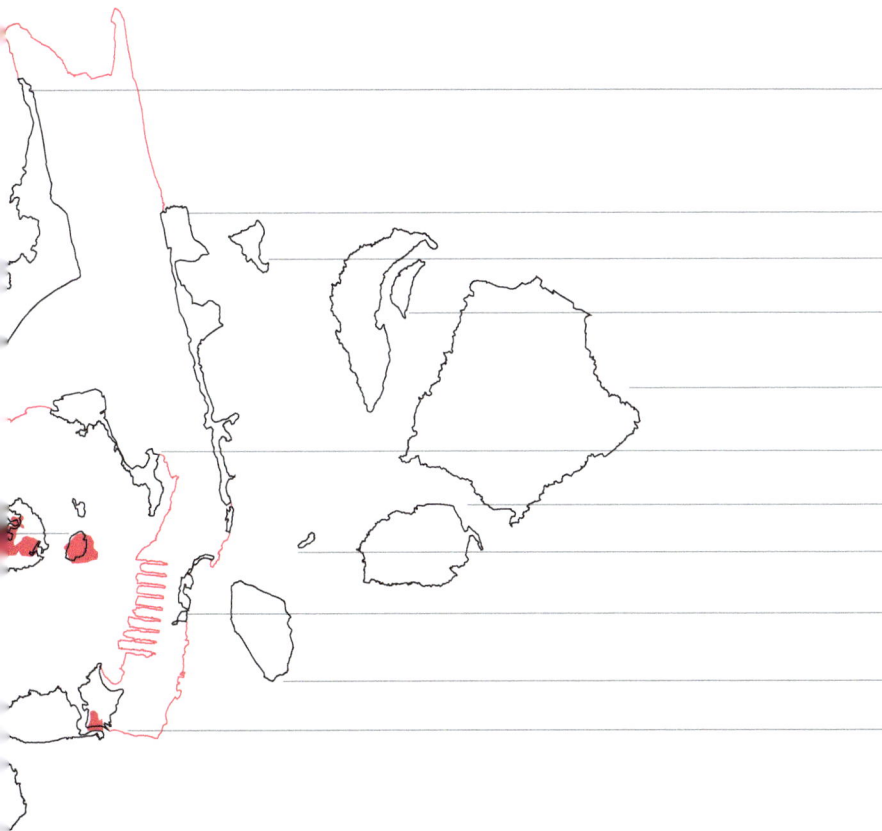

BLACK BANK 103 ACRES

JACKS HOLE CR 53 ACRES

BROAD CREEK 10 ACRES

EAST HIGH MEADOW 95 ACRES

JO CO 395 ACRES

GOOSE POND 30 ACRES

SILVER HOLE 84 ACRES

WINHOLE HASSOCK 1 ACRES

BROAD CHANNEL EAST 5 ACRES

SUBWAY ISLAND 48 ACRES

BIG EGG 59 ACRES (~2.5 RESTORED)

	BIG EGG MARSH 2003	ELDERS POINT MARSH, EAST 2006	ELDERS POINT MARSH, WEST 2009-2010

image source: David Harmon, 2003

image source: Galvin Brothers Inc., 2006

image source: Galvin Brothers Inc., 2009

	BIG EGG MARSH	ELDERS POINT MARSH, EAST	ELDERS POINT MARSH, WEST
ACRES OF SALT MARSH:	~2.5	43	40
CUBIC YARDS OF SAND:	7,500	248,500	302,000
MATERIAL PLACEMENT:	Thin layer dispersal	Pipe slurry and fine graded	Pipe slurry and fine graded
PLANTING METHODS:	Low marsh peat pots	Low marsh plugs and pots High marsh transition plugs and pots	Transplanted low marsh hummocks Transplanted upland materials High marsh plugs
COST:	Construction Cost: $tk	Construction Cost: $17,237,126 (Costs do not include sand placement, USACE labor or monitoring)	Total contract cost: $11,948,300 (Cost does no include USACE labor and monitoring)
PARTNERS:	National Park Service	USACE and PANY/NJ (Mitigation for the NY/NJ Harbor Deepening Project)	USACE, NYSDEC, NYCDEP, PANYNJ

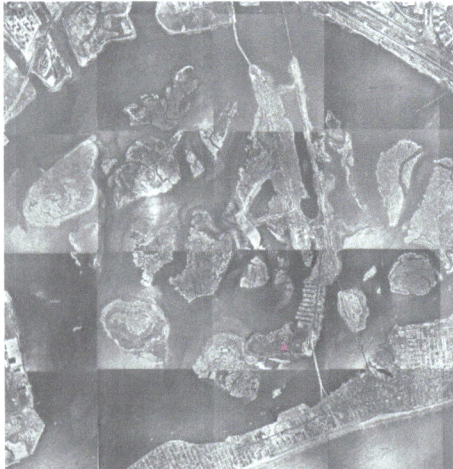

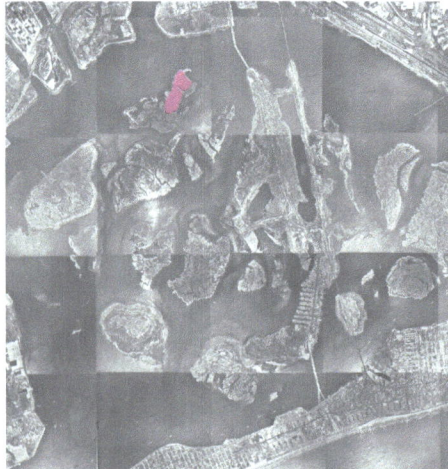

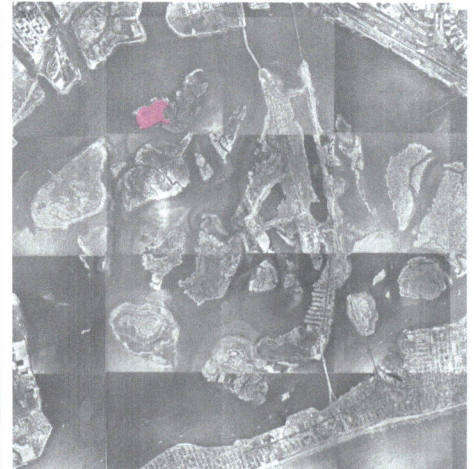

aerial image source: New York State Department of Environmental Conservation, 1974

YELLOW BAR HASSOCK 2012	BLACK WALL MARSH 2012	RULERS BAR HASSOCK 2012

image source: US Army Corps of Engineers, 2012	image source: American Littoral Society, 2012	image source: American Littoral Society, 2012
46	20	10
375,000	150,000	92,000
Pipe slurry and fine graded	Rough graded	Rough graded
Transplanted low marsh plant hummocks High marsh and high marsh transition plants Seed dispersal	Seed dispersal	Low marsh plugs
Total Project Costs: $19,642,857 (Includes labor and monitoring)	Marsh Contract Cost for Black Wall and Rulers Bar: $705,000	Marsh Contract Cost for Black Wall and Rulers Bar: $705,000
USACE, NYSDEC, NYCDEP, PANYNJ, NPS, American Littoral Society, Jamaica Bay Ecowatchers, US Fish and Wildlife Service	USACE, NYSDEC, NYCDEP, PANYNJ, NPS, American Littoral Society, Jamaica Bay Ecowatchers, Jamaica Bay Guardian, US Fish and Wildlife Service	USACE, NYSDEC, NYCDEP, PANYNJ, NPS, American Littoral Society, Jamaica Bay Ecowatchers, Jamaica Bay Guardian, US Fish and Wildlife Service

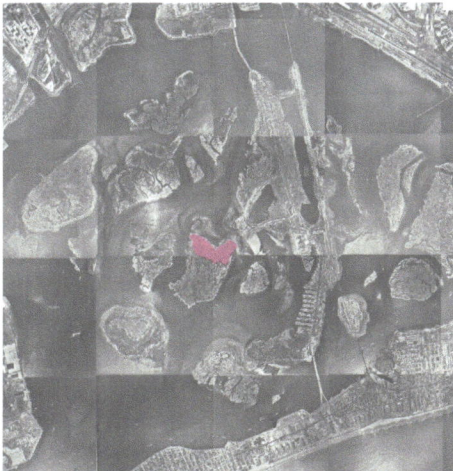

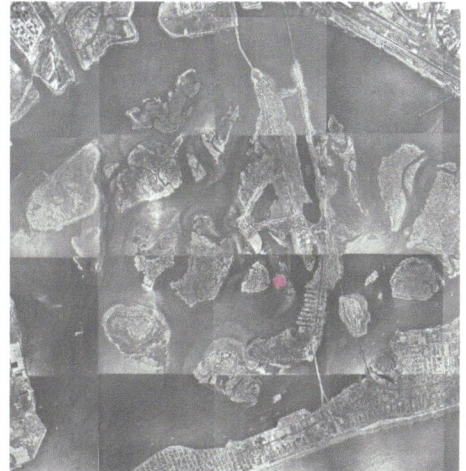

BIG EGG MARSH

2003

Tidal Wetlands 1974

☐ Intertidal Marsh
☐ High Marsh
◼ Coastal Shoals, Bars and Mudflats

SCALE

AREA ~2.5 acres salt marsh habitat

VOLUME 7,500 cubic yards of sand

SOURCE Deep, narrow trench 22ft wide by 6ft deep excavated via swing ladder dredge from adjacent tidal creek (less impact on benthic habitat than wide, shallow excavation)

FUNDING

COST unknown

PARTNERS 100% National Park Service funded, implemented by Gateway National Wildlife Refuge with Cooperative Ecosystem Studies Unit at University of Rhode Island and over 200 volunteers

MATERIAL HANDLING

PLACEMENT Thin layer dispersal

High pressure slurry "rainbowed" onto site through 20 inch intake pipe to 10 inch outflow nozzle

Dredge slurry was sprayed up to 130ft distance (least impactful dispersal method) aimed to increase elevation a minimum of 8 inches above the highest existing *Spartina alterniflora* tussock (targeted areas received up to 40 inches of fill)

Finished elevation designed so most of marsh would be inundated twice daily at high tide, minimizing risk of colonization by *Phragmites australis*

STABILIZATION Hay bale and plastic fence silt runoff containment

image source: George Frame, 2003

image source: George Frame, 2005

REVEGETATION METHODS

PLANTING >20,000 *Spartina alterniflora* peat pots planted 50 cm (19.69 in) apart beginning October, 2003

Plants grown at NYCDPR Native Plant Center from seed harvested at two Staten Island locations 6 - 18 miles from Jamaica Bay

65ft x 65ft cells created with plastic fencing and flagging strung overhead to deter geese from landing and eating new plants

MONITORING

TECHNIQUES Three SETs at both experimental and control site read at three month intervals
30 permanent 1m square vegetation plots
100 grid markers with elevations
16 2m square unplanted plots
Survey birds, mammals, insects, spiders
Water quality, water table and soils monitored

FINDINGS Spring 2004 nearly 100% planting survival rate with seedling density from natural germination of *S. alterniflora* up to 800 seedlings per 10 sq feet (highest density in wet depressions)

After one growing season silt and algae covered the sand and marsh was being colonized by native macroinvertebrates

Significant wave erosion along NW edge (200 foot strip 10-20 feet wide lost 8-16 inches elevation) and SE edge (65 foot strip 15 feet wide lost 8 inches elevation)

Preexisting *S. alterniflora* survived only with < 8 inches of fill

After one year geese became habituated to fences and swim through breaks at high tide to eat plants

BIG EGG MARSH

aerial imagery

image source: New York State Department of Environmental Conservation

1974

image source: Google Earth

2013

ELDERS POINT MARSH, EAST

2006

Tidal Wetlands 1974

Intertidal Marsh

High Marsh

Coastal Shoals, Bars and Mudflats

SCALE

AREA   42.69 acres salt marsh habitat restored

VOLUME   248,500 cubic yards of sand

SOURCE   157,500 cu yds sand dredged from Rockaway Inlet
46,000 cu yds sand dredged from Ambrose Channel
45,000 cu yds Amboy Aggregates purchased material

FUNDING

COST $13,000,000 (mitigation for harbor deepening Port Authority of New York and New Jersey)

PARTNERS   USACE and PANY/NJ

image source: Galvin Brothers Inc, 2006

REVEGETATION METHODS

PLANTING   580,000 plugs / 46,000 pots *S. alterniflora* (low marsh)

33,640 tri-plugs (*S. alterniflora, D. spicata, S. patens*)

Plugs planted 18" OC and grown from local seed stock by the National Resources Conservation Service (NRCS)

MONITORING

RESOURCES $2 million for five years

FINDINGS   2010 nest of Diamondback Terrapins found

S. alterniflora growth is consistant with control site (JoCo marsh)

No significant sediment loss or gain except on west side of island where elevation has decreased slightly, probably due to sediment transport and accretion north along sand spit

image source: Galvin Brothers Inc, 2006

MATERIAL HANDLING

PLACEMENT   Stockpile at Floyd Bennett Field

Pipe slurry and GPS machine fine graded

STABILIZATION   Coir (coconut jute mat) toe stabilization

40 acres of 50ft x 50ft waterfowl barrier cells with two years of maintenance

image source: Galvin Brothers Inc, 2006

ELDERS POINT MARSH

aerial imagery

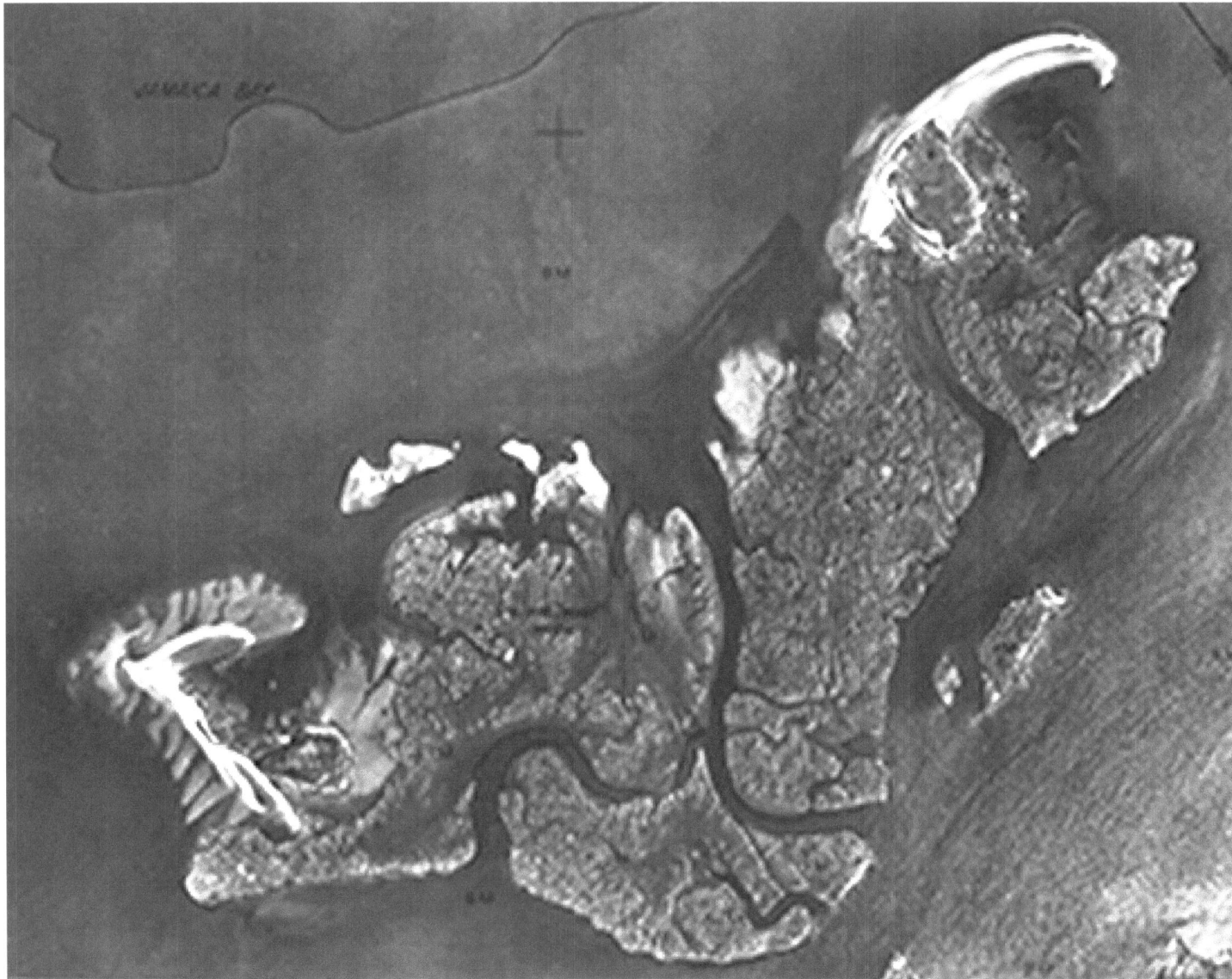

source: New York State Department of Environmental Conservation, 1974

1974

image source: Google Earth

2003

ELDERS POINT MARSH, EAST

restoration planting plan

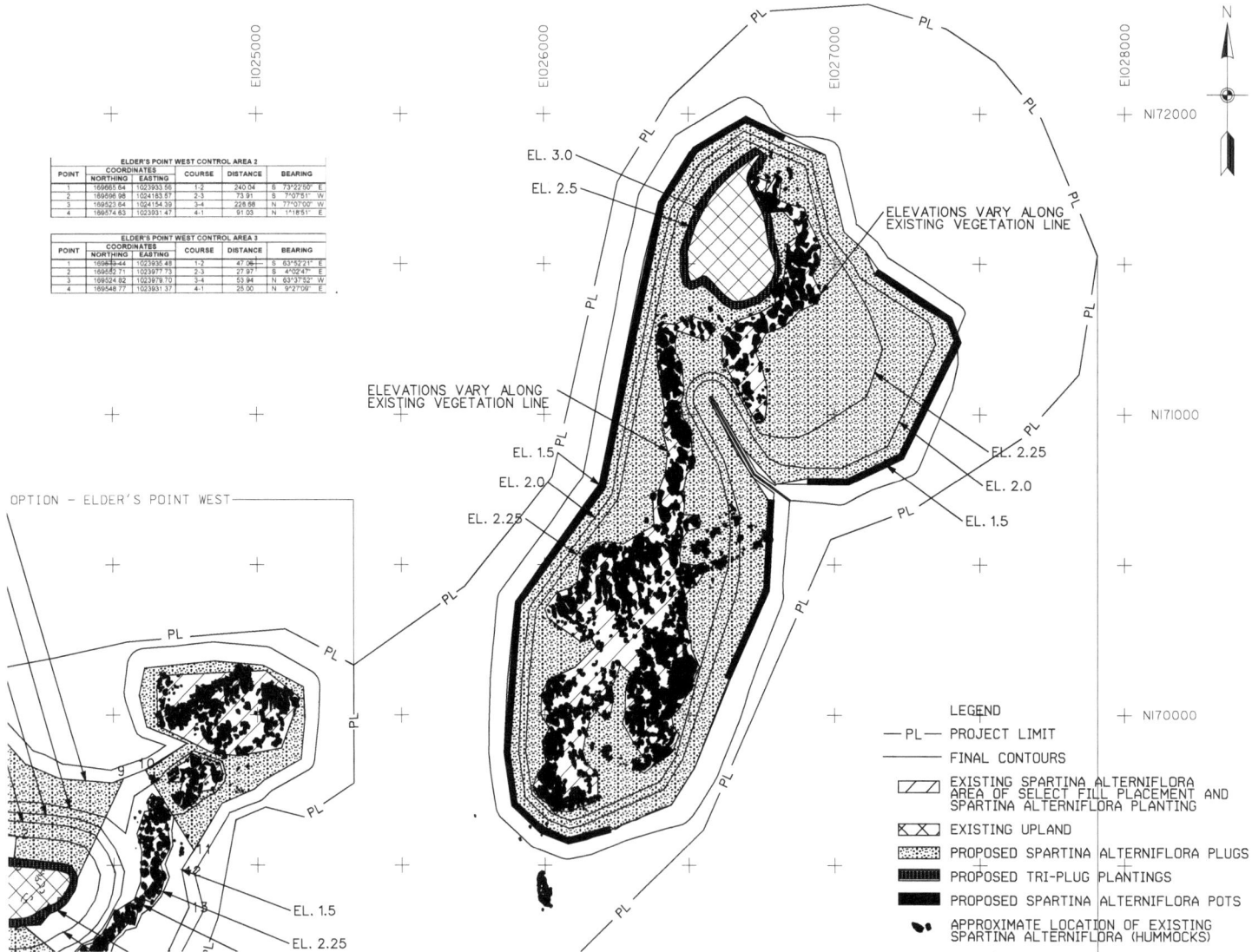

ELDER'S POINT WEST CONTROL AREA 2

| POINT | COORDINATES | | COURSE | DISTANCE | BEARING |
	NORTHING	EASTING			
1	169665.64	1023933.56	1-2	240.04	S 73°22'50" E
2	169596.98	1024183.57	2-3	73.91	S 7°07'51" W
3	169523.64	1024154.39	3-4	228.68	N 77°07'00" W
4	169574.63	1023931.47	4-1	91.03	N 1°18'51" E

ELDER'S POINT WEST CONTROL AREA 3

| POINT | COORDINATES | | COURSE | DISTANCE | BEARING |
	NORTHING	EASTING			
1	169513.44	1023935.48	1-2	47.06	S 63°52'21" E
2	169582.71	1023977.73	2-3	27.97	S 4°02'47" E
3	169524.82	1023979.70	3-4	53.94	N 63°37'52" W
4	169548.77	1023931.37	4-1	25.00	N 9°27'09" E

EI025000
EI026000
EI027000
EI028000

N172000
N171000
N170000

N

EL. 3.0
EL. 2.5
EL. 2.25
EL. 2.0
EL. 1.5

ELEVATIONS VARY ALONG
EXISTING VEGETATION LINE

ELEVATIONS VARY ALONG
EXISTING VEGETATION LINE

EL. 1.5
EL. 2.0
EL. 2.25

OPTION – ELDER'S POINT WEST

EL. 1.5
EL. 2.25

LEGEND

— PL — PROJECT LIMIT

FINAL CONTOURS

EXISTING SPARTINA ALTERNIFLORA
AREA OF SELECT FILL PLACEMENT AND
SPARTINA ALTERNIFLORA PLANTING

EXISTING UPLAND

PROPOSED SPARTINA ALTERNIFLORA PLUGS

PROPOSED TRI-PLUG PLANTINGS

PROPOSED SPARTINA ALTERNIFLORA POTS

APPROXIMATE LOCATION OF EXISTING
SPARTINA ALTERNIFLORA (HUMMOCKS)

source: US Army Corps of Engineers

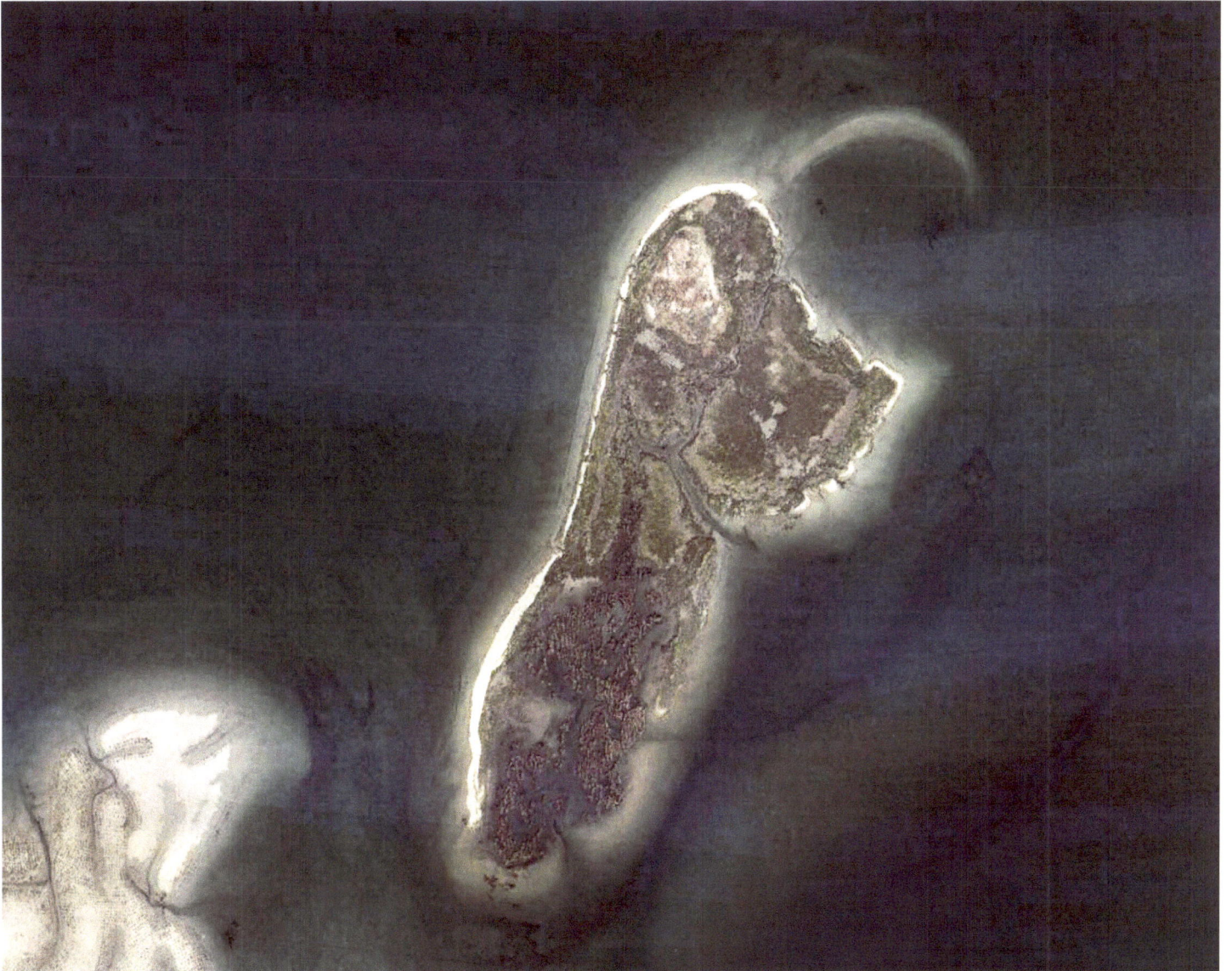

2013

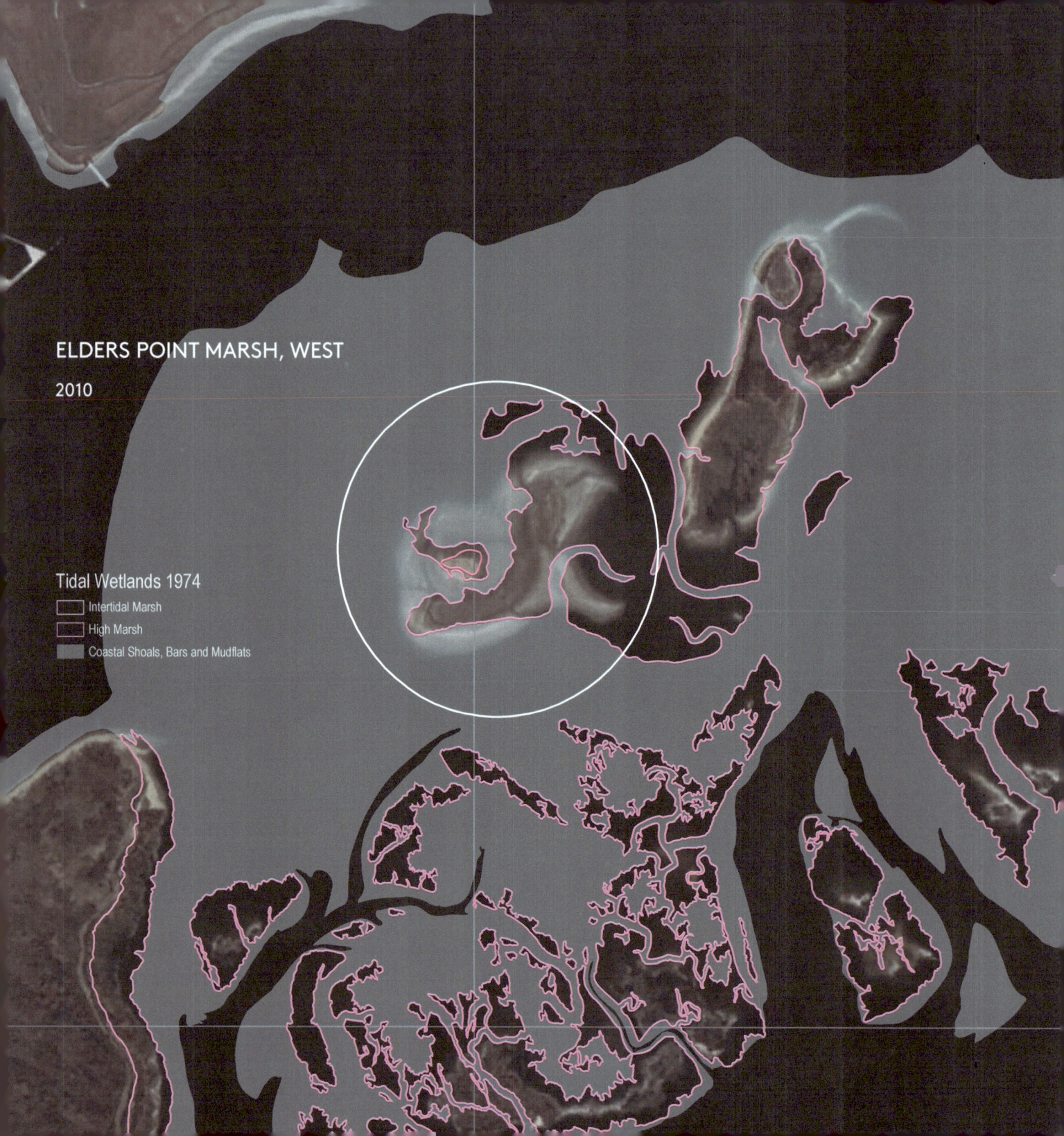

ELDERS POINT MARSH, WEST

2010

Tidal Wetlands 1974

Intertidal Marsh

High Marsh

Coastal Shoals, Bars and Mudflats

SCALE

AREA   ~ 40 acres salt marsh habitat restored

upland	1.22 acres
high marsh	4 acres
low marsh	19 acres
side slopes	16 acres

VOLUME   302,000 cubic yards of sand

SOURCE   Dredged from Ambrose Channel NY/NJ Harbor
Deepening Project

FUNDING

COST $17,200,000 ($11,650,000 sand / $5,620,000 marsh)
Continuing Authorities Program (CAP) 204/207 under the
Harbor Deepening Project

65% federally funded; 35% non-federal (NYSDEC, NYCDEP)

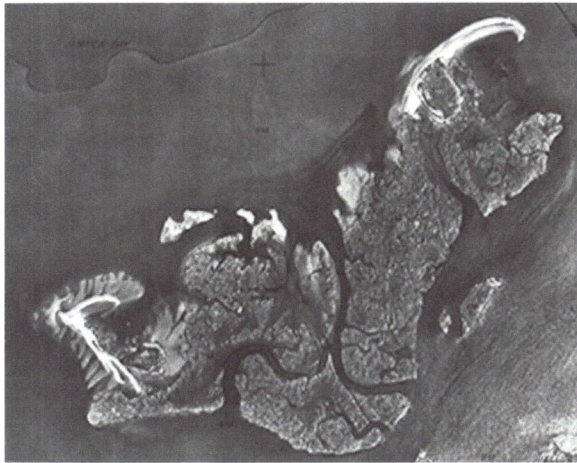

image source: US Army Corps of Engineers

MATERIAL HANDLING

PLACEMENT   Hopper dredge, pipe slurry and GPS machine fine graded

STABILIZATION   No toe stabilization

MONITORING

RESOURCES $2 million for five years

FINDINGS   S. alterniflora growth is consistant with control site
(JoCo Marsh at eastern side of Jamaica Bay)

No significant sediment loss or gain

source: New York State Department of Environmental Conservation, 1974

REVEGETATION METHODS

TRANSPLANT   7,689 transplanted *S. alterniflora* hummocks
(all low marsh plantings were transplanted on site, no
plugs or pots)

Native upland plant material salvaged from Gerritsen
Creek Restoration Project

NEW PLANTINGS   USDA NRCS Cape May Plant Materials Center provided
upland beach plumb shrubs grown from GNRA seed stock

High marsh (4 acres) 69,909 plants

Bookbinder style plugs for high marsh transition zone
(4 acres) 85,580 plants hand fertilized and planted in hole
dug by gas powered auger

image source: US Army Corps of Engineers

ELDERS POINT MARSH, WEST

restoration planting plan

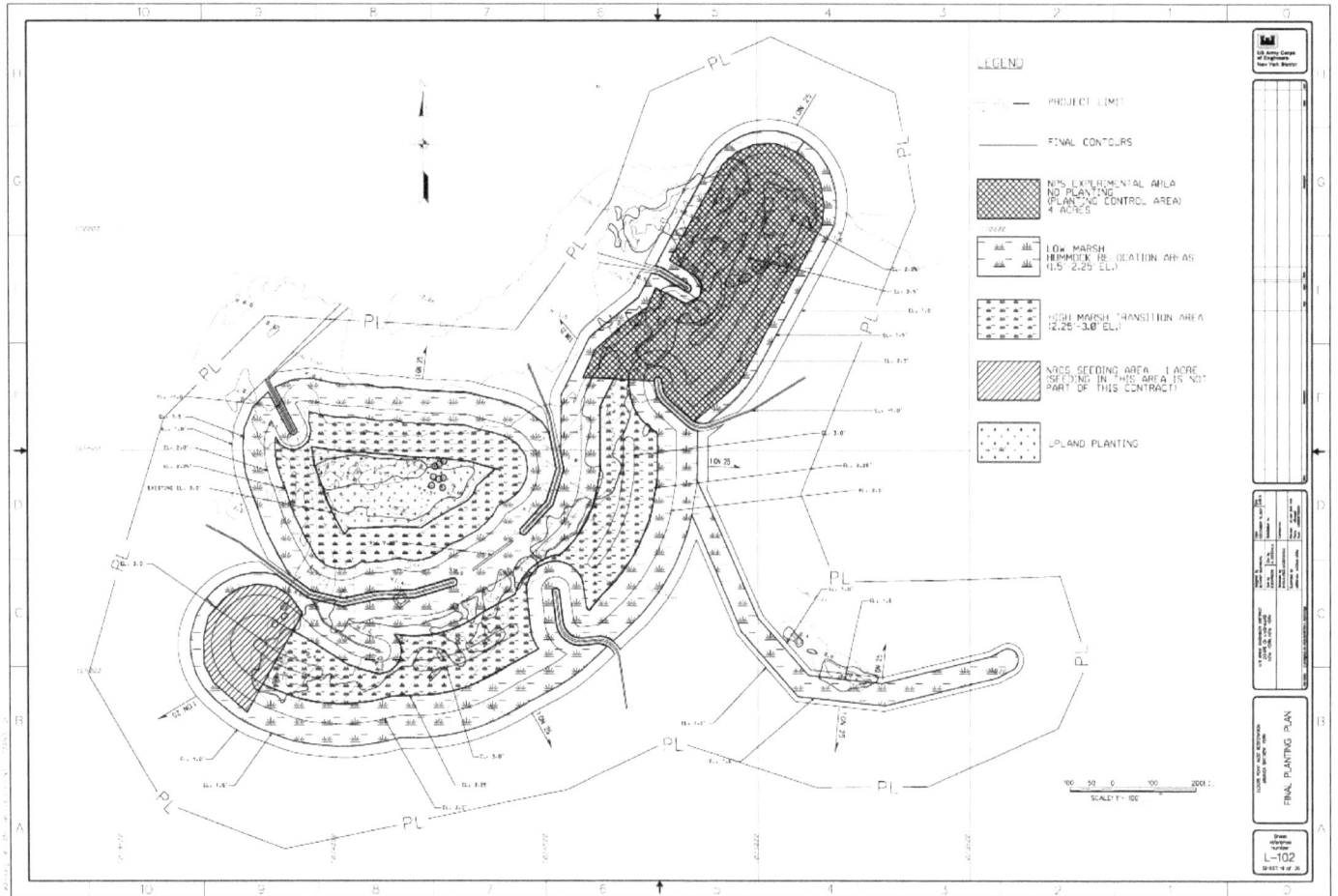

source: US Army Corps of Engineers

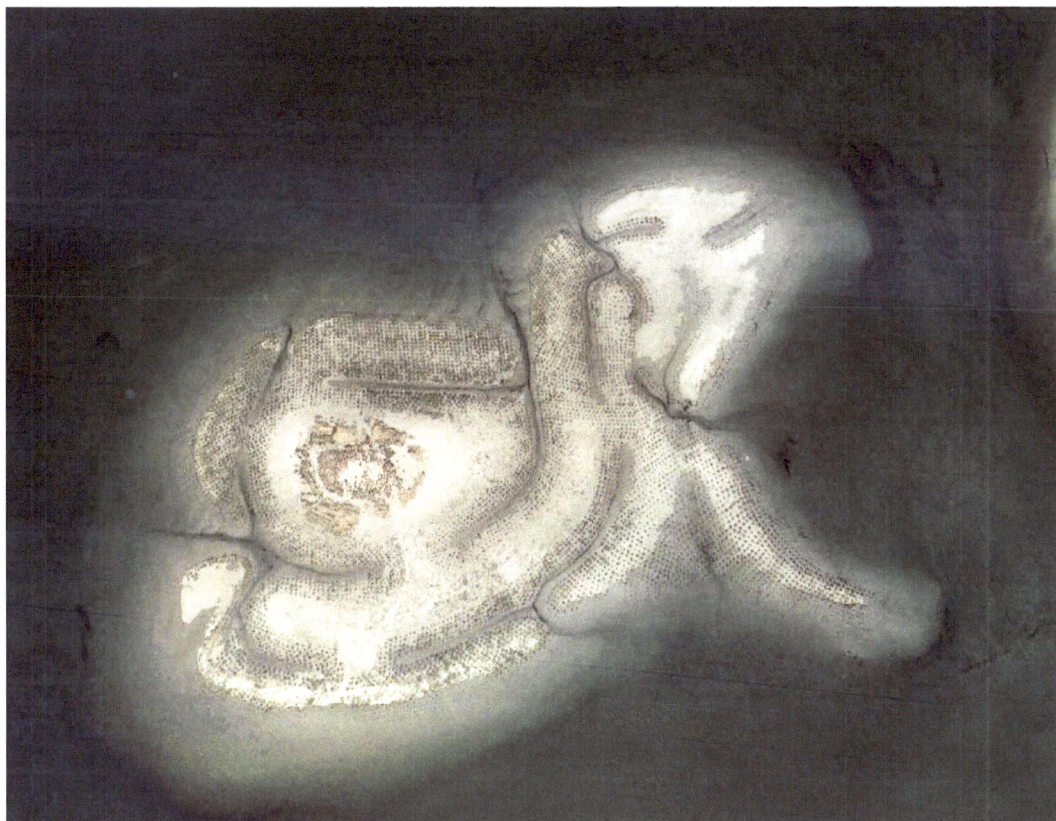

image source: Google Earth
2013

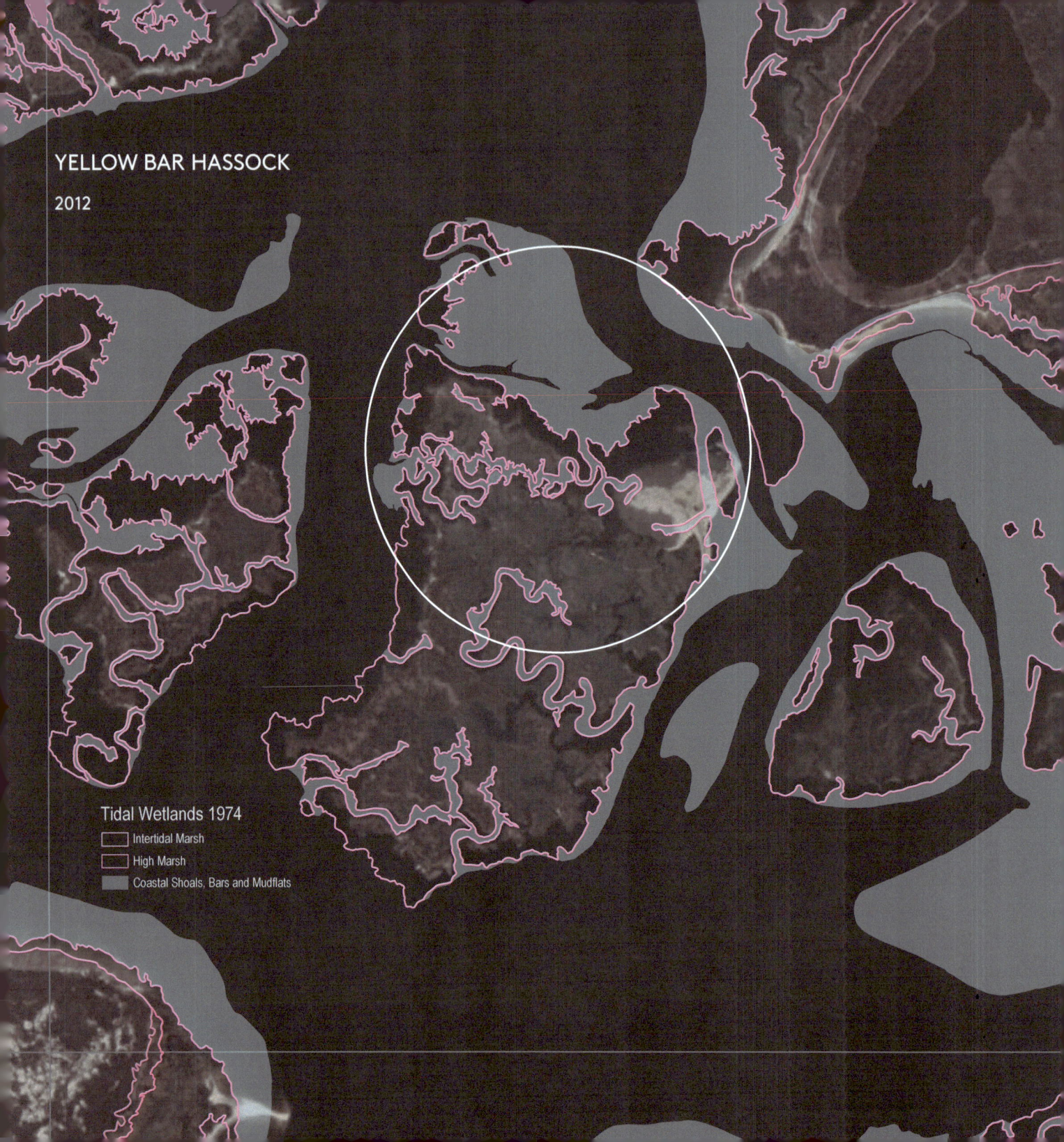

YELLOW BAR HASSOCK

2012

Tidal Wetlands 1974

☐ Intertidal Marsh
☐ High Marsh
■ Coastal Shoals, Bars and Mudflats

SCALE

AREA

45.537 acres salt marsh habitat restored
~13.1 acres transplanted low marsh hummocks
~28 acres low marsh seeding

VOLUME

375,000 cubic yards of sand

SOURCE

Ambrose Channel dredging (Continuing Authorities Program (CAP) 204/207 under the Harbor Deepening Project)

FUNDING

COST

$ 19,642,857 (Total costs include Sandy repairs)

PARTNERS

65% federally funded
35% local share (NYSDEC, NYCDEP and PANYNJ)

image source: Melissa Alvarez, USACE, 2012

MATERIAL HANDLING

PLACEMENT   Hopper dredge, pipe slurry, GPS machine fine graded

image source: U.S. Army Corps of Engineers, 2012

image source: Lisa Baron, USACE, 2012

REVEGETATION METHODS

PLANTING

13.36 acres transplanted low marsh hummocks

17,175 high marsh plants planted on 4.427 acres

21,859 low-high marsh transition plants

350 lbs low marsh smooth cordgrass seed dispersal over 27.75 acres

image source: Melissa Alvarez, USACE, 2012

YELLOW BAR HASSOCK

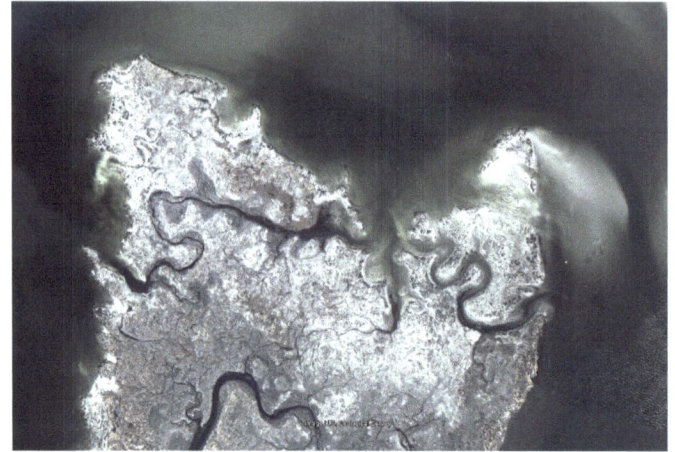

Restoration planting plan
source: US Army Corps of Engineers

2009

2012

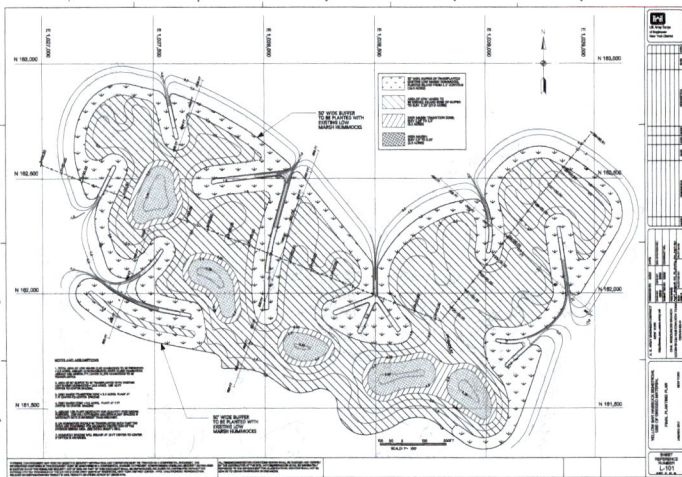
2014

image sources: Google Earth

image source: USACE / Great Lakes Dredge & Dock - Gregg Kohl, Gregg Kohl Photography Inc.

2012

BLACK WALL MARSH
2012–2013

Tidal Wetlands 1974

☐ Intertidal Marsh
☐ High Marsh
▨ Coastal Shoals, Bars and Mudflats

SCALE

AREA   ~20.5 acres salt marsh habitat restored

VOLUME   150,000 cubic yards of sand

SOURCE   Ambrose Channel dredging
(New York/New Jersey Harbor Deepening Project)

image source: Ecowatchers, 2013

image source: Ecowatchers, 2013

MATERIAL HANDLING

PLACEMENT   Hopper dredge, pipe slurry, GPS machine rough grade

REVEGETATION METHODS

PLANTING   Locally harvested Spartina alterniflora seed dispersal over 14.5 acres

FUNDING

COST $2,100,000 (Sand placement costs only)

PARTNERS   USACE, NYSDEC, NYCDEP and PANYNJ
Sand placement 100% funded by NYSDEC and NYCDEP

Community based planting partners: NYCDEP, American Littoral Society, Jamaica Bay Ecowatchers, Jamaica Bay Guardian

image source: Ecowatchers, 2013

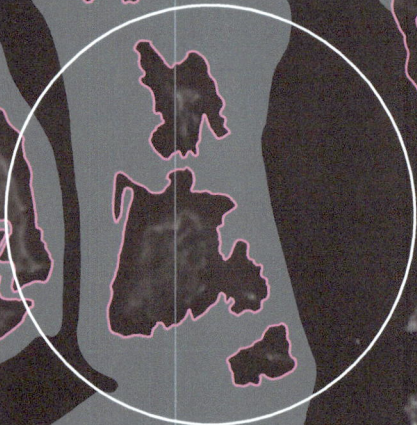

RULERS BAR HASSOCK

2012–2013

Tidal Wetlands 1974

☐ Intertidal Marsh

☐ High Marsh

■ Coastal Shoals, Bars and Mudflats

SCALE

AREA   ~9.8 acres salt marsh habitat restored

VOLUME   95,000 cubic yards of sand

SOURCE   Ambrose Channel dredging
            (New York/New Jersey Harbor Deepening Project)

image source: Ecowatchers, 2013

REVEGETATION METHODS

PLANTING   In Fall 2012, 150 lbs of Spartina alterniflora seed
            were gathered by local volunteers and sent to NRCS in
            Cape May. In the spring volunteers planted 88,000
            Spartina alterniflora plugs over 8 acres.

image source: Ecowatchers, 2013

MATERIAL HANDLING

PLACEMENT   Dump and rough grade

FUNDING

COST $1,311,000 (sand placement costs only)

PARTNERS   NYSDEC, NYCDEP and PANYNJ
            sand placement 100% funded by NYSDEC and NYCDEP

            Community based planting partners: NYCDEP, American
            Littoral Society, Jamaica Bay Ecowatchers, Jamaica Bay
            Guardian

image source: Ecowatchers, 2013

BLACK WALL MARSH, RULERS BAR HASSOCK

aerial imagery

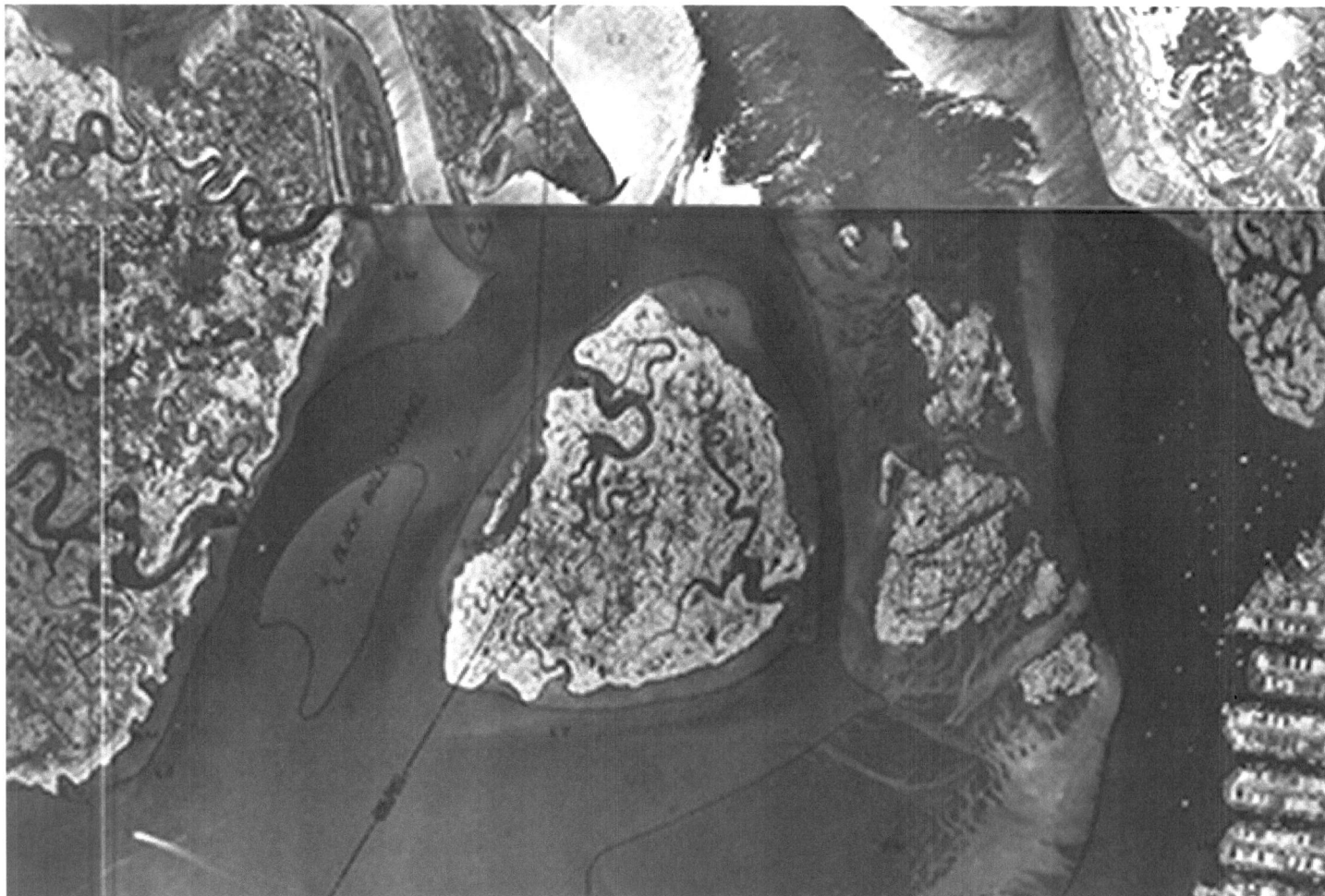

image source: New York State Department of Environmental Conservation

1974

image source: Google Earth
2012 pre-restoration

image source: Google Earth
2013

www.ingramcontent.com/pod-product-compliance
Lightning Source LLC
Chambersburg PA
CBHW060827270326
41931CB00002B/87